86th U.S. Open

Shinnecock Hills

Writer
Marino Parascenzo

Photographers
Brian Morgan
Jim Moriarty

Editor
Bev Norwood

ISBN 0-9615344-1-9

©1986 United States Golf Association®
Golf House, Far Hills, New Jersey 07931

Statistics produced by Burroughs Corporation

Published by International Merchandising Corporation,
One Erieview Plaza, Cleveland, Ohio 44114

Designed by Marti Shattuck, Moran Printing Company, Orlando, Florida 32809

Printed in the United States of America

This is the second in a series of Annuals on the United States Open Championship and, coincidentally, this year marked the second playing of the Championship at Shinnecock Hills. The first, ninety years ago, was a far different occasion.

In 1896, the National Open had been held only once previously, and there were but thirty-five entries. There seemed to be as many challenging for the lead midway of this year's final round, before Raymond Floyd gained his decisive advantage with a birdie at the sixteenth hole.

Raymond's victory at age 43 made him the oldest winner of the Championship. We on the senior side of the game have had our eyes on this promising youngster for a long time.

My friends at Rolex are donating the proceeds from sales of this book through the USGA Associates Program to benefit junior golf. Income will assist the USGA in its efforts to promote junior golf at its member clubs and elsewhere throughout the United States, thereby helping to ensure the future of this great game.

Arnold Palmer

Arnold Palmer

86th U.S. Open

June 12-15, 1986, Shinnecock Hills Golf Club, Southampton, New York

Contestant	Rounds				Total	Prize
Raymond Floyd	75	68	70	66	279	$115,000.00
Lanny Wadkins	74	70	72	65	281	47,646.00
Chip Beck	75	73	68	65	281	47,646.00
Lee Trevino	74	68	69	71	282	26,269.00
Hal Sutton	75	70	66	71	282	26,269.00
Ben Crenshaw	76	69	69	69	283	19,009.00
Payne Stewart	76	68	69	70	283	19,009.00
Jack Nicklaus	77	72	67	68	284	14,500.75
Bernhard Langer	74	70	70	70	284	14,500.75
Mark McCumber	74	71	68	71	284	14,500.75
Bob Tway	70	73	69	72	284	14,500.75
Denis Watson	72	70	71	72	285	11,870.00
Greg Norman	71	68	71	75	285	11,870.00
Mark Calcavecchia	75	75	72	65	287	11,028.00
David Frost	72	72	77	67	288	8,884.66
Fuzzy Zoeller	75	74	71	68	288	8,884.66
Craig Stadler	74	71	74	69	288	8,884.66
Gary Koch	73	73	71	71	288	8,884.66
Joey Sindelar	81	66	70	71	288	8,884.66
Jodie Mudd	73	75	69	71	288	8,884.66
Bobby Wadkins	75	69	72	72	288	8,884.66
David Graham	76	71	69	72	288	8,884.66
Scott Verplank	75	72	67	74	288	8,884.66
Dave Eichelberger	80	70	72	67	289	6,461.80
Andy Bean	76	72	73	68	289	6,461.80
Don Pooley	75	71	74	69	289	6,461.80
Calvin Peete	77	73	70	69	289	6,461.80
Larry Mize	75	71	73	70	289	6,461.80
Larry Rinker	77	71	70	71	289	6,461.80
Severiano Ballesteros	75	73	68	73	289	6,461.80
Tom Watson	72	71	71	75	289	6,461.80
Lennie Clements	75	72	67	75	289	6,461.80
Mike Reid	74	73	66	76	289	6,461.80
Paul Azinger	78	72	70	70	290	5,575.00
Tom Kite	74	74	73	70	291	5,170.20
Philip Blackmar	75	75	70	71	291	5,170.20
Larry Nelson	75	73	70	73	291	5,170.20
John Cook	75	73	70	73	291	5,170.20
*Sam Randolph	79	71	68	73	291	Medal
Mark McNulty	75	72	68	76	291	5,170.20
Mark O'Meara	76	73	71	72	292	4,566.00
Bruce Fleisher	76	73	71	72	292	4,566.00
Roger Maltbie	76	70	73	73	292	4,566.00
Doug Tewell	74	73	71	74	292	4,566.00
Kenny Knox	72	76	74	71	293	3,963.00

Contestant	Rounds				Total	Prize
Dave Barr	75	73	73	72	293	3,963.00
Sandy Lyle	78	71	72	72	293	3,963.00
Mark Lye	80	70	70	73	293	3,963.00
Johnny Miller	76	72	71	74	293	3,963.00
David Hobby	76	74	71	73	294	3,427.00
Barry Jaeckel	75	74	71	74	294	3,427.00
Mac O'Grady	75	69	73	77	294	3,427.00
Tsuneyuki Nakajima	72	72	78	73	295	3,092.00
Bill Glasson	76	74	69	76	295	3,092.00
Hubert Green	75	75	75	71	296	2,914.50
Bill Israelson	79	71	72	74	296	2,914.50
Greg Powers	80	70	72	74	296	2,914.50
Wayne Levi	77	70	74	75	296	2,914.50
Frank J. Conner	75	73	77	72	297	2,791.00
Chen Tze Chung	76	72	75	74	297	2,791.00
Peter Jacobsen	76	72	73	76	297	2,791.00
Rick Fehr	72	77	75	74	298	2,761.00
Jeff Sluman	75	74	75	74	298	2,761.00
David Ogrin	76	73	74	75	298	2,761.00
Richard Mast	76	74	76	74	300	2,761.00
Howard Twitty	79	71	75	76	301	2,761.00
Andy North	79	71	77	75	302	2,761.00
Michael Malaska	74	74	80	75	303	2,761.00
Peter Oosterhuis	78	70	78	78	304	2,761.00
Bradford Greer	78	72	79	76	305	2,761.00

Chen Tze Ming	74-77—151	Brett Upper	79-74—153	Gene George	76-81—157
Tom Pernice, Jr.	80-71—151	Dave Rummells	78-76—154	Miller Barber	80-77—157
Hale Irwin	77-74—151	Thomas Byrum	81-73—154	*Brian Watts	82-75—157
Donnie Hammond	78-73—151	Wayne Smith	77-77—154	Tom Sieckmann	77-81—158
Chris Perry	75-76—151	Buddy Gardner	82-72—154	Cleve Coldwater	77-81—158
Bob Murphy	79-72—151	Fred Wadsworth	81-73—154	Steve Gotsche	81-78—159
Mark Brooks	75-76—151	Scott Simpson	78-76—154	Corey Pavin	80-79—159
Thomas Cleaver	77-74—151	Jack Lewis	77-77—154	Andrew Magee	82-77—159
Bill Rogers	75-76—151	Jeff Maggert	81-73—154	Ray Cragun	84-75—159
Dan Pohl	79-72—151	Jerry Haas	80-74—154	Walt Chapman	82-78—160
*Tim Fleming	76-75—151	Jay Haas	78-77—155	Ed Dougherty	82-78—160
Joe Inman, Jr.	79-72—151	Tom Lehman	78-77—155	Bill Sakas	86-75—161
Don Reese	74-77—151	Mike Gove	78-77—155	Rick Schuller	85-76—161
Bob Lohr	73-78—151	Curtis Strange	76-79—155	Gary Krueger	84-77—161
Tim Simpson	78-74—152	Jim Albus	79-76—155	Frederick Funk	84-77—161
John Mahaffey	79-73—152	John Adams	79-76—155	Scott Williams	83-78—161
Rafael Alarcon	81-71—152	Greg Farrow	83-72—155	Douglas Campbell	86-76—162
Jim Thorpe	79-73—152	George Burns	83-72—155	*Bob Lewis, Jr.	83-79—162
Danny Edwards	83-69—152	Jeff Lewis	79-76—155	Perry Arthur	85-77—162
Ronnie Black	78-74—152	Mike Hulbert	81-74—155	Barney Thompson	80-83—163
Tracy Nakazaki	82-70—152	Roy Biancalana	78-77—155	Jim Smith	86-78—164
Donald Dubois	74-78—152	Bob Pancratz	78-77—155	Lee Chill	86-78—164
Bobby Clampett	81-72—153	Cary Hungate	79-77—156	*John Daly	88-76—164
Ossie Moore	78-75—153	Kirk Triplett	78-78—156	Stanley Utley	80-86—166
Adrian Stills	78-75—153	Michael Colandro	80-76—156	Bob Eaks	85-86—171
Mark Pfeil	79-74—153	Bob Gilder	76-80—156	Jerry Pate	WD
David Thore	79-74—153	Evan Schiller	82-74—156	Ken Green	82 WD
Bruce Zabriski	77-76—153	Mike Smith	81-75—156	Jack Renner	85 WD
Brad Fabel	79-74—153	John Thomas McGinnis	83-73—156		

Professionals not returning 72-hole scores received $600 each.

*Denotes amateur.

86th U.S. Open
Shinnecock Hills

Gentlemen, this beats rifle shooting. It is a game I think might go in our country.
William K. Vanderbilt

Shinnecock is what golf should be like if it were invented today.
Frank Hannigan

History has a warped sense of humor. A man named John Sutter was digging for a completely unglamorous reason when he came up with those yellow pebbles in California. Archimedes was merely trying to take a bath. And Columbus was hell-bent for Asia.

Young Willie Dunn wasn't quite in the same league, but in his small way, he also changed history. Dunn merely hit a few golf shots in France. They landed on Long Island, New York.

The year was 1889. Dunn, a Scottish golfer and course architect, was busy laying out a golf course at Biarritz, the famous French spa. A trio of well-heeled Americans dropped by — William K. Vanderbilt, Edward S. Mead and Duncan Cryder. They were interested in this odd game they had heard so much about. Would Mr. Dunn show them how it works? Dunn took them to the "chasm hole," a 125-yarder across a deep ravine, and proceeded to knock a few balls onto the green. To men looking for ways to fill their ample leisure time, it looked like more fun than almost anything.

"Gentlemen," Vanderbilt is said to have told his companions, "this beats rifle shooting. It is a game I think might go in our country."

With this thought in mind, the Americans persuaded the skeptical Dunn — he thought golf had a far better future in France — to come to the United States and do one of these golf courses for

Frank Hannigan surveys Shinnecock Hills.

them. And so Shinnecock Hills Golf Club was born, and much of American golf along with it. Dunn arrived in March of 1891, and by that summer, golf was being played on Shinnecock Hills. On July 18, 1896, the second United States Open was played there. But not before it almost died there.

Ninety years and eighty-five playings later, the U.S. Open returned to Shinnecock Hills. The field was more than four times larger than the original thirty-five players, and the purse immensely larger, at some $700,000. But to peer back ninety years through history's gauzy curtain does more than measure the Open's progress. It fills in some blanks in golf history. Golf had been known in the United States for years. Yet the game had only coughed and sputtered. And then it caught in the late 1880s, principally in a tiny corner of the Northeast. The geography was no real surprise. Golf had flourished where the money was, that's all. But the timing: Why in the late 1800s? Why not before, or later?

Well, until fussy historians and disputatious social philosophers take up the question, it seems safe to say that golf happened when and where it did simply because it was an idea whose time had come.

These were the "Gay Nineties," a time of incredible growth and change. America was like a kid awkwardly growing up, with his hair slicked down and his shirttail hanging out. The U.S. was changing inexorably from a vast agricultural society to a mighty industrial empire that was sucking people into the great urban centers like fierce whirlpools.

If Jules Verne could have invented a satellite, what a picture it would have sent back: to the east, the wealthy enjoying the maddening charms of the hook and the slice; to the west, the last Indian warparty plodding its weary way into history. Elsewhere in the world, forces had just been loosed that would shape the Twentieth Century: Hitler and Einstein were boys, Lenin and Gandhi young men, and Angelo Roncalli a youthful seminarian,

Previous page, 16th green (foreground), 9th green, and the clubhouse. Above, Hole 1.

many years from taking the name John XXIII.

Vanderbilt was right. This game would go in our country.

But not for everybody just yet. It was Everyman's game in Scotland, where it was born, but in the U.S. only the rich played golf. No mystery there. Only the rich could afford the equipment, only the rich had the leisure time, and it was the rich who built and owned the golf courses. This should explain, if nothing else does, why golf in the U.S. became known as "the rich man's game." The tag had staying power. It has stuck to golf despite the fact that guys rush off from their service stations and mills to get in a quick nine before dark at nearly eight thousand five hundred public courses throughout the country.

Shinnecock Hills, at Southampton, was nothing if not a rich man's course. It was part of the playground of the wealthy who summered in that clutch of Long Island communities known collectively as "The Hamptons." Shinnecock Hills was not the first golf course in the U.S. (there is some dispute about which one was), but it might have been the most influential, setting the pattern for practically all clubs of the future. It was the first to incorporate, the first to build a clubhouse and the first to have a waiting list. It even had a separate course for women. For a while.

Willie Dunn arrived early in 1891, bent on getting a course down for these Americans and getting back to France. Dunn and Samuel Parrish, one of Shinnecock's founding members, went scouting for their course. They found it near Southampton, in the Shinnecock Hills, a stretch of rolling, brush-covered sand dunes overlooking Peconic Bay to the north. It was as close to the Scottish linksland as Dunn was likely to find in the U.S. Dunn recruited a crew of some one hundred and fifty Indians from the nearby Shinnecock reservation, and except for a couple of horse-drawn roadscrapers, the course was cut by hand through grasping blueberry bushes and boulders. Play began in the fall of 1891.

Dunn's original course was a twelve-holer. It quickly became crowded. So the members had him put in a nine-hole

Hole 3, par 4, 453 yards.

course for women, in order — the history books say — to relieve congestion on the twelve-hole course. But note that the nine-hole course was not meant to catch overflow from the main course. It was for the ladies. Next, picture the ladies in their ankle-length dresses, broad-brimmed hats, parasols and polite sitting-room swings, picking their way around the course. That ought to suffice for a working definition of "congestion."

Nice try, but the ladies insisted on playing in the fast lane. So Dunn was sent back to the drawing board. A single eighteen-hole course emerged in 1892, according to club historians.

Most of the nation's golf clubs, Shinnecock Hills among them, flowered in the ritzy, high-priced circles of the Northeastern Seaboard. They were much like a club of clubs. The next and natural step was a competition of some kind among them. The United States Golf Association was about to be born. Not out of mere necessity, but sheer exasperation. Thanks to a man who didn't know the meaning of the word defeat. He was — but only in the spirit of first causes — the father of the USGA.

This was Charles Blair Macdonald of Chicago, builder of the Chicago Golf Club and, eventually, the National Golf Links, next door to Shinnecock Hills. Macdonald, a big mustachioed man, was perhaps the finest American amateur of his day. He was the clear favorite when the Newport Golf Club of Newport, Rhode Island, scheduled the first "national" championship for September 1894. But he lost when, in the second round, his topped shot came to rest against a stone wall running across the fairway. It cost him a two-stroke penalty. He had had no objection to the stone wall in the first round, when he took a four-stroke lead. But now he argued that a proper golf course does not have a stone wall in the fairway. Not only that, but amateur championships traditionally are held at match play. So the nation's first amateur championship didn't take.

Neither did the second, a month later, in October 1894, at St. Andrews in Yonkers, New York. It was held at match play, as Macdonald had insisted. But he lost again. This time he argued that this had merely been an invitational tournament.

Hole 17, par 3, 172 yards.

A real championship, he said, had to be staged by a real organization.

By now the group was totally exasperated. So they decided to meet all of Macdonald's terms. First, they would form a national organization. On December 22, 1894, at the Calumet Club in New York, representatives of five clubs met: Shinnecock, Newport, St. Andrews, Chicago Golf Club and The Country Club of Brookline, Massachusetts. They called their organization the Amateur Golf Association (it would be changed later to the American Golf Association, and finally the United States Golf Association). And they scheduled their championship, the first U.S. Amateur, for October 1-3, 1895, at Newport. There was nothing left for Macdonald to do but win it, and he did.

The Americans, following the lead of British golf, held an "Open" along with the Amateur. With amateurs the prime golfers of the day, the Open was a kind of tag-along event that gave the professionals something to do. Horace Rawlins, a transplanted Englishman and assistant pro at Newport, won that first Open — and the $150 first prize and $50 gold medal — against a field of nine other pros and one amateur. The U.S. Open was on its way. Next stop: Shinnecock Hills, where a rich and enlightened man helped make yet another piece of history.

A piece of it came into view in the 1981 U.S. Open, when burly Jim Thorpe took the first-round lead. Instantly, the press corps pronounced Thorpe the first black ever to lead a U.S. Open. They were wrong by eighty-five years. That distinction dated back to the second U.S. Open, on July 18, 1896, at Shinnecock Hills. And it belonged to one John Shippen.

But who on earth was John Shippen, and how did a black man get into the Open in 1896? Thus begins one of the most fascinating tales in golf, and one almost buried in history.

John Shippen, the first black leader.

The 1896 Open drew thirty-five entries, most of them transplanted Scottish and English pros who had emigrated to jobs at the new U.S. clubs. Two of the entrants were Shippen, a black man (or Negro then), and Oscar Bunn, a Shinnecock Indian, both caddies at Shinnecock Hills. The pros threatened to walk out if those two played.

Enter Theodore A. Havemeyer from Newport Golf Club and the first president of the USGA. Havemeyer uttered some magic words to the dissidents, and the Open was on. There are two accounts of what he said. One holds that he soothed the angry pros by telling them that Shippen actually was only half-Negro, that his mother was an Indian.

"And that isn't true, either," said Mrs. Clara Shippen Johnson, daughter of John Shippen. She's 76 now, and lives in a nursing home in Glendale, Arizona, and she still gets angry when she hears that story.

"Because," she said, "those other men also objected to Oscar Bunn, and Oscar Bunn was a Shinnecock Indian. It wasn't only my father they wouldn't play with. It was Oscar Bunn, too."

Much of golf history still describes Shippen as a half-black, half-Indian. This irritates Mrs. Johnson.

"My father was a Negro," she says, an edge coming to her soft voice. "Every time I meet somebody, I have to correct that story." She corrects it with this brief family history:

The Rev. John Shippen (her grandfather), a Presbyterian minister, and his wife were both black. They had four daughters and two sons (one of them John), and they lived in Anacostia, Maryland, near Washington, D.C. The Rev. Shippen became the minister on the Shinnecock reservation and moved the family there.

The confusion over young John Shippen's origin apparently comes from the phony Havemeyer tale, or from Shippen's own marriage. "My mother was a full-blooded Indian," Mrs. Johnson said.

At all events, the slight didn't bother Shippen. "Dad said he was used to it," Mrs. Johnson said. And so he ignored it.

Havemeyer, however, did not, even though the Open was in danger. A boycott would have killed it for 1896. And with the pros angry, the Open might have been badly damaged for years to come. He spoke his magic words anyway.

"We will play the Open with you," he told the rebellious pros, "or without you."

They played. Shippen shot a 78 in the first round, tying for the lead with four others, including eventual champion James Foulis, a Scottish pro from the Chicago Golf Club. Shippen's chances died in the second round at the thirteenth hole when he put a ball on a sandy road. Had the sand wedge been invented in time, the U.S. Open might have had its first black champion. But it hadn't, and Shippen spent a lifetime getting the ball out. He took an eleven on the hole — seven strokes over par, precisely the distance between Foulis and him at the end.

James Foulis, 1896 U.S. Open champion.

Shippen tied for fifth at 78-81 — 159. Bunn finished twenty-first at 89-85 — 174.

Shippen went on to play in other Opens, and spent most of his life in golf. He died at age 90 in a nursing home near Newark, New Jersey, a poor man.

"I'm sure my father's whole life would have been different," Clara Shippen Johnson said, "if he hadn't got into that road."

It was a different Shinnecock Hills for the 1986 Open. Golf had outgrown the original, so in 1931 the noted architect, William Flynn, was called in. He virtually remade the course. One of his key employees was a young man named Dick Wilson, who would go on to become one of the finest Course architects in the land.

History next came calling in the person of USGA official Harry Easterly, who suggested the Open be played there. Frank Hannigan, now the USGA Senior Executive Director, had fallen in love with Shinnecock at the 1977 Walker Cup Match. Hannigan and Easterly came up with a scheme.

"Shinnecock," Hannigan said, "is what golf should be like if it were invented today."

But there was a bit of a problem. Generally, the host club stages the Open, handling the zillion details — parking, transportation, gallery marshals, hot dogs. Shinnecock, a "summer club," does not have what might be called a resident membership. So the USGA would have to rent Shinnecock and put on the Open itself. Golf's equivalent of, say, the Normandy Invasion. And just as successful.

On behalf of the United States Golf Association, I would like to welcome you to Great Britain, for the first playing of the British Open in the United States.
William J. Williams

The United States Golf Association was reaching for a little history when it put the 1986 U.S. Open at Shinnecock Hills. It took a step back in time, and drew a bridge across the Atlantic Ocean to the cradle of the game. Or, as USGA President William J. Williams put it at his Wednesday morning press conference, with a wry grin:

"On behalf of the United States Golf Association, I would like to welcome you to Great Britain, for the first playing of the British Open in the United States."

No one missed the point. A look at Shinnecock was enough: the gently rolling hills, sandy soil, short, scrubby growth nodding and sometimes whipping in the sea breezes. There it was — a British-style course on Long Island, New York. Then there were the ghosts of the past — Willie Dunn, Samuel Parrish, Charles Blair Macdonald, John Shippen — all hovering in benign interest. This Open had a patina unlike any through the previous eighty-five playings. This one fairly glowed.

And it had the requisite cast. Youth was represented by Scott Verplank, a brilliant amateur who had turned pro just before the Open. There were the kings of the game — Spain's Severiano Ballesteros and West Germany's Bernhard Langer — and the struggling Tom Watson, who hadn't won in nearly two years.

Then there was the over-the-hill gang, which refused to be written off. Jack Nicklaus, the four-time Open champion, launched the "Year of the Oldies" in

American sports when he raced to the Masters title in April at age 46. There was the ever-young Lee Trevino, also 46, touchy back and all. There was Raymond Floyd, the kid of this group at age 43.

In the starting field of one hundred and fifty-six golfers, two stood out: Nicklaus and Australian Greg Norman, the hottest golfer in the world. Norman had two victories, two seconds, and a tenth in his previous five starts. Nicklaus was the 1986 candidate to win golf's Grand Slam — the Masters, U.S. Open, British Open and PGA Championship. No one had ever won all four in a single year. But when Nicklaus was the man with the chance, people were talking.

Two months earlier, on the Edenic stretches of Augusta National Golf Club, on a balmy Thursday in April, Nicklaus was an elder statesman of the game. He hadn't done much for a long time. He last won at the 1984 Memorial Tournament, and before that, the 1982 Colonial National. Beyond that, you had to go back two more years, to 1980, when he won both the Open and the PGA.

But that was history. In 1985, Nicklaus missed the cut in the Open at Oakland Hills after having made twenty-one straight. He also missed the cut in the British Open. He was struggling. He was saying the right things but doing the wrong ones. Before the Masters, an Atlanta newspaperman wrote what everyone was thinking, that Nicklaus was through, washed up, done. Nicklaus did not enjoy reading his obituary.

So on that Sunday in April, after he had wrapped up his record sixth Masters — and his first since 1975 — he said the right thing again. This time, at the unlikely age of 46, he said with a satisfied chuckle: "I told you so."

Nicklaus came to this Open with that old glint in his eye. He had vindicated himself, and he was looking at the Grand Slam, a sight probably no man should presume to see.

"I don't think the Grand Slam is a likely

Previous page, Jack Nicklaus. Above, other "Oldies" Lee Trevino (left) and Raymond Floyd.

thing to happen," Nicklaus said. "But obviously, when you're in position, you do everything you can to give yourself a chance to win it. I'd kick myself if I didn't."

The closest anyone ever came to the Slam was Ben Hogan in 1953. He won the Masters, U.S. Open and British Open, then did not play in the PGA. The next closest was Nicklaus himself, in 1972. He took the first two legs, then his bid died when Trevino beat him in the British Open at Muirfield.

Nicklaus' 1986 Masters victory did more than give him his twentieth major and a chance at the Slam. It remade the face of American golf instantly.

Steel, cars, electronics and the like weren't the only things feeling the invasion by foreign interests. International golf had come fast. It was merely cresting at the 1985 Open at Oakland Hills. Remember that finish? Chen Tze Chung of Taiwan, who led most of the way, Canada's Dave Barr and Zimbabwe's Denis Watson — any one of them could have won it. Only the clutch play of lanky Andy North kept the trophy in America. And while foreign golf was rising, American golf reached a plateau. A high one, but a plateau nevertheless. American golf needed a focal point, a hero. Nicklaus would do fine. But who expected it?

Halley's Comet was passing by the Earth at the time of the Masters. Nicklaus was like that. Everybody looked up when he came roaring down the stretch at Augusta, barging by Norman, Spain's Severiano Ballesteros and American Tom Kite. In short, anyone who happened to be in his way. Like the old days. And that week, at Oak Hill, Baltusrol, Winged Foot, Inverness, Oakmont — all famous clubs emerging from a golf-starved winter — the new season took off like a rocket.

Norman tied for second in the Masters. A week later, he also tied for second. He won his next outing two weeks later for his first U.S. victory since 1984. Three

Foreign threats included No. 1 money winner Greg Norman of Australia (previous page), Bernhard Langer of West Germany (left) and Seve Ballesteros of Spain (right).

Prologue

Defending champion Andy North.

weeks later, a tie for tenth, and the next week, another victory.

Norman was a favorite of American fans the instant he hit the U.S. tour in 1983. Much was expected of his long, powerful game — a major, for instance.

"It is just a matter of when," he has often said. He had come close. He lost to Fuzzy Zoeller in a playoff for the 1984 Open. At the 1986 Masters, just a stray shot at the final hole kept him from at least a tie with Nicklaus.

And so the Open arrived with golf anchored by Nicklaus at one corner and flapping in the winds of change everywhere else.

There was Ballesteros, victim of four straight near-misses in Europe after crashing at the Masters. He was choking at the memory, they said. Then he won the British Masters the Sunday before coming to Shinnecock. Was he a favorite? "There are so many good players over here," he said, shrugging, "and over there." Tom Watson was winless for nearly two years. The difference between winning and not winning, he said, was the difference between walking uphill and walking downhill. "I'm playing well enough to win," he said. "I'm just not putting." And so it went. But it always came back to Nicklaus and the Masters victory.

Andy North, the 1985 Open champion, was a spectator at the Masters. His injured right hand was in a cast. He phoned Nicklaus that Sunday night.

"Tell me the truth, Jack," North said, recounting the conversation. "Doesn't it feel great to win after what people had been saying about you?"

"Yeah, it sure did," Nicklaus said.

"Now you know how I felt," North said. "You were written off for only a month. I've been written off for seven or eight years."

And so the parade went by. Everyone agreed that it was a great idea, bringing the Open back to Shinnecock; that the course would be a stern test, but a fair one; that it was wild, lovely and unspoiled.

86th U.S. Open

Tsuneyuki Nakajima and the Japanese press.

Arnie's Army marched on.

A new bridge provided easy access, as did express trains from New York City.

86th U.S. Open
First Round

We've had wind from all four directions in four days of practice. If there's a fifth direction, this is it.
                                            Lanny Wadkins

I've got room reservations — in a padded cell.
                                            Jack Renner

If I had made that little putt at the eighteenth, I'd been happy with a 76.
                                            Jack Nicklaus

"Welcome to the British Open..." USGA President Bill Williams had said. Everybody said this would be a transplanted British Open, coming to Shinnecock Hills. But this was stretching things a bit far.

The U.S. Open got under way on a day when you could measure the wind by the number of junked umbrellas in the trash barrels, and by shivering spectators trying to pull their heads into their windbreakers. From the start, the day was dark under a profoundly sullen sky, and there were two things uncertain about the wind: the direction, which was from anywhere, and the buffeting gusts up to thirty miles an hour or so. Otherwise, the wind was more or less constant at fifteen to twenty-five miles an hour all the livelong day.

"We've had wind from all four directions in four days of practice," said Lanny Wadkins, who finished in a crowd at 74. "If there's a fifth direction, this is it."

Then there was the temperature, of course. After a balmy, sunny Wednesday, it had dropped into the fifties. The wind-chill factor made it seem worse. And then there was heavy rain that even delayed play for fourteen minutes in the after-

Bob Tway led on a cold, rainy first day.

First Round

noon. It was generally agreed that this was one of the worst days in memory at an Open.

So, if Blue Point oysters made pearls, Bob Tway had found one. Tway, 27, one of America's most promising young players, took Shinnecock for a par 70. He had played early, when the weather was merely awful. It was the first time since Gary Player shot par 70 in the 1974 Open at Winged Foot that par was not broken on the first day. Tway's 70 held up for a one-stroke lead over Greg Norman.

"This was kind of a survival day," Tway said, in muted awe. "With conditions like this, you could blow yourself right out of the tournament." A heavy rainstorm swept in at that instant, at 1 p.m., and the din on the roof of the press tent drowned him out. "I didn't think it could get much worse," Tway said, raising his voice. "But it just did."

First Round

Bob Tway	70
Greg Norman	71
Kenny Knox	72
Tom Watson	72
Denis Watson	72
David Frost	72
Rick Fehr	72
Tsuneyuki Nakajima	72

"Survival" was the right word. He turned in par 35, a figure that looks deceptively simple. He birdied the 453-yard par-four third with a twenty-foot putt, and the 367-yard par-four eighth after dropping a wedge shot to one foot. He bogeyed at the 408-yard par-four fourth and the 447-yard par-four ninth, both of which he failed to reach in two. He was brilliant with his par saves — from a bunker at the first hole, a ten-foot putt for his five at the fifth, and a four-footer for his three at the sixth.

He had to do a lot of saving to come in with another 35. From four feet at the par-four tenth, from three at the par-three seventeenth, and from ten feet at the 450-yard eighteenth. He got to two under with back-to-back birdies, a two at

First Round

the eleventh on a twenty-foot putt, and a three at the twelfth from twenty-five feet. Then the course brought him back to even on quick bogeys, a five at the fourteenth after he drove into the rough, and a five at the fifteenth, where he was bunkered.

Norman kept the pressure on. Having pretty well recovered from a respiratory ailment that had plagued him since early in 1985, he came into the Open with two victories, two seconds and a tenth in his previous five starts.

"Which holes played differently because of the wind?" came the question.

"One through eighteen," Norman cracked.

He also suffered a "survival" day. He saved par eight times with a dazzling greenside game from bunkers and rough that left him putts of one to ten feet. Norman three-putted from the fringe for a bogey-five at the third hole, but got back to even par with a twenty-five foot birdie putt at the par-five fifth. Then he came to the ninth. It's a grueling 447-yard par four. Here's what it measured playing into the stiff wind: Even Norman, one of the biggest hitters around, failed to reach it in two. He bogeyed, and turned at one over par. He halved his differences with the back nine, offsetting a bogey from the bunker at the fifteenth, with an eighteen-foot birdie-two at the seventeenth.

"My 71," Norman said, "was the equivalent of a 66 or 67." The ninth hole gave up only two birdies all day, and produced one hundred and two bogeys and eighteen double bogeys, playing to an average of 4.88, and it was only the second-toughest hole on the course. The eighteenth, a par four of 450 yards, was the real brute —three birdies, sixty-seven bogeys, twenty-seven double bogeys or worse, and an average of 4.91.

The Open seemed safe from the Oldies. Jack Nicklaus shot a whopping 77, Lee Trevino 74 and Raymond Floyd 75. Floyd's

Greg Norman (left) shot 71 while Kenny Knox (right) was among those with 72s.

performance put some teeth in a comment Tom Watson had made earlier. Someone asked Watson to pick a favorite. "Just look at who's been playing well for a few weeks coming into the Open," Watson advised.

Floyd had been tied for the lead at the Westchester Classic the week before the Open, but a final-round 77 swept him out of the picture. He survived the first round of the Open with a solid 75, if you can call a 75 solid. On the day of double bogeys, he had only one, a six at the ninth hole. It capped a no-birdie front nine. He bogeyed the third and fourth. His game flickered to life on the back nine, where he offset three bogeys with a pair of birdies at the eleventh and thirteenth.

Denis Watson, who tied for second in 1985, and David Frost, Japan's Tsuneyuki (Tommy) Nakajima and Tom Watson, the 1982 champion, solved Shinnecock with 72s.

Jack Renner solved Shinnecock by walking out.

When he came into the old clubhouse, he found a note on his locker. It had to do with room reservations.

"I've got room reservations," Renner said, "in a padded cell." He began packing.

"I shot an 86 today and didn't get any bad breaks. I deserved every one of them. This," he added, speaking of the weather, "is why I don't play the Crosby (now the Pebble Beach National Pro-Am, notorious for bad weather). I'm nobody's fool. I wait 'til the Open to shoot my 86 — when I'm front and center." (Actually, Renner shot an 85. He just didn't know it.)

It seemed the Grand Slam was safe for another year. "If I had made that little putt at the eighteenth," Nicklaus said, "I'd been happy with a 76."

Nicklaus arrived at Shinnecock on his game. He almost won his own tournament, the Memorial, late in May, with a burst of six straight birdies on the final

Tsuneyuki Nakajima of Japan (left) and Denis Watson of Zimbabwe also posted two-over scores.

First Round

nine. But he had an unruly driver here, and that's an unforgiving thing in such wind. He made the turn in 36, one over. Then he got flattened. Double bogeys add up fast, and he made three of them and shot 41. The toughest to take was at the tenth, where a gust of wind caught him on his backswing and kept him there. "I never even saw the ball," he said. It disappeared into the dense scrub on the right, and despite a horde of hunting spectators, he couldn't find it. It was his first lost ball, he said, since the 1959 British Amateur. And it turned up anyway. He was already heading back toward the tee when someone shouted. But he thought his five minutes had expired, and he continued to the tee. Later, he said he was unsure whether he had time left.

It was a moot point, however. His lie was such that he might not have been able to hit the ball without taking a drop. At the thirteenth, he was short in two and three-putted from twelve feet. At the eighteenth, he missed the fairway and pitched out over the fairway. There went three sixes.

"Here's the story," Nicklaus said. "I hit four greens, needed only twenty-six putts, and shot 77," he said. "I can't remember when I hit so few greens in regulation."

His 77 left him in good company. When the eighteen players left on the course completed their rounds the next morning, the average for the first round was 77.55. And that didn't include Renner's 85.

David Frost of South Africa was in the third-place tie.

It was the kind of day that spawned odd events.

Ken Green, the Marble Dale, Connecticut pro whose caddie is his sister, Shelley, came without a windbreaker. He had no credit cards and no cash, and so he could not buy one. And the folks at the pro shop wouldn't extend him credit. He looked at his sister, snuggled in her jacket.

"It's your job," he said, "to get wet."

Shelley shot him a flinty glance. "No way," she said. "Don't even think about it."

Jack O'Leary, a *Boston Herald* golf writer, took off his jacket and gave it to Green. O'Leary then had to buy a sweatshirt. Green shot 82.

Then there was a historic wrong-ball case. The victim was Fred Wadsworth, 23, a pro from Fort Benning, Georgia. He hooked his drive under a small, dense tree at the third hole. It was in grass, and he had to get on his knees to hit it out. First, he identified it: a Titleist 384, 90 compression, No. 4. He had put three pencil dots under the 4. He swung, and all his ball did was pop up, hit a limb and come back down. Or so he thought. Actually, his ball had gone through the thick growth and out onto the fairway. The ball that popped up had been sitting right under his ball. Unaware, he swung again. He got the alien ball out to the fairway, and then discovered his error. Hitting the second ball cost him a two-stroke penalty. Cruelly enough, the second ball was precisely the same make and model as his own, right down to the 4. "Unbelievable," Wadsworth said.

86th U.S. Open

Jack Nicklaus shot 77 with a lost ball off the tee at No. 10.

86th U.S. Open
Second Round

A ten-shot lead would not be comfortable.
        Greg Norman

Look, you're trying to do too much with the ball. Why don't you just go back to hitting it straight.
      Pete Bender, Norman's caddie

You gotta remember one thing: Shoemaker wasn't carrying that horse. That horse was carrying him.
        Lee Trevino

 Well now, this was more like it.
 The sun broke through on Shinnecock at mid-morning. The leaden skies and raw punishment of Thursday were gone. The temperature came up some twenty degrees, to the high seventies, and the winds died down to mere zephyrs, out of the friendly south instead of the hostile north. Holes that couldn't be reached with two driver shots on Thursday — the ninth, for example — now were within reach. "There's not enough wind to hurt you today," Lee Trevino noted. "Maybe enough to help you. Against the wind, it's maybe a half-a-club difference, and downwind, maybe one club."
 With the warming came the blossoming of hope, but it was only marginal for four-time Open champion Jack Nicklaus. Thoughts of a Grand Slam for 1986 were still alive, but only barely. Nicklaus stumbled down the back nine on four bogeys and three birdies for a 72 that left him at 149 — nine over par and ten strokes off the lead. "Well, conditions made nine, ten and eighteen par fours again," Nicklaus said. "But I didn't do much. I drove better, but still not well. Finally made some birdies. Three of them. Led our

Second Round

group — two-day total."

Nicklaus was not amused, but he found enough spirit to chuckle at himself. "I'm not excited about the 72," he said. "It should have been 68 or 69. But I would think that if I shoot just under par tomor-

Second Round

Greg Norman	68-139
Lee Trevino	68-142
Denis Watson	70-142
Raymond Floyd	68-143
Bob Tway	73-143
Tom Watson	71-143

row, and have a good round Sunday, I'll still have a good chance."

The best chance, however, was in the big hands of Greg Norman, the stark-blond Australian and runnerup to Fuzzy Zoeller in the 1984 Open. Norman carved himself the distinction of becoming the first player in history to complete two Open rounds at Shinnecock under par. Also the only one. Norman posted a two-under-par 68 for a thirty-six-hole total of one-under 139. That gave him a three-stroke lead. There were still thirty-six holes to play, yet the question came: Was a three-stroke lead comfortable?

"A ten-shot lead would not be comfortable," Norman said.

His lead might have been cushier had he not run afoul of the tenth hole. In a way, Norman was a victim of the better conditions. The 409-yard hole, so intimidating on Thursday, now was within easy reach. So easy that it tempted Norman into using a three-iron off the tee. He hooked his drive into the rough, came up short with a five-iron approach, chipped on and two-putted for his bogey five. Until that point, he was five strokes ahead of first-round leader Bob Tway, who was on his way to a 73-143. The bogey chipped one stroke off his lead, and another bogey at the thirteenth — where he went from rough to bunker — lopped off yet another.

Norman had seemed about to knock old Shinnecock silly. He tore through the front nine with a no-bogey 31. He had an

Except at No. 10, Greg Norman played steadily to a three-shot lead.

elegant short game. He needed just nine putts. He birdied the first hole from fifteen feet, the fourth from one foot, the fifth from twelve, and the eighth from five. If the tenth was the start of something bad, his caddie stopped it post haste.

"There was nothing wrong with using the three iron off the tee," Norman said. "I was just trying to do too much with the ball. I wanted to get down to the bottom of the hill, to get a level lie, and I tried to hook the shot."

That's when Norman's caddie, Pete Bender, stepped in. Ordinarily, caddies are meant to be seen and not heard, more so even than children. But Norman said that an alert caddie can be invaluable. "So Pete has the freedom to speak," Norman said. And Pete spoke.

"He told me," Norman said, "Look, you're trying to do too much with the ball. Why don't you just go back to hitting it straight." It was a statement, not a question. That settled Norman down. Except for the bogey at the thirteenth, he made his way home in solid if disappointing pars.

And he found an old friend just astern — Lee Trevino.

Trevino had shot a 74 in the numbing first round. He barged back into the chase for his third Open title with a 68 and was joined by Denis Watson (70) at 142, three behind Norman. The thought was delicious: Could yet another "Oldie" win in 1986.

Trevino was reminded that Nicklaus had won the Masters in April at age 46, and that Willie Shoemaker at age 54, had won the Kentucky Derby with Ferdinand. So, could Trevino win the Open at 46?

"You gotta remember one thing," Trevino said, cackling. "Shoemaker wasn't carrying that horse. That horse was carrying him."

Raymond Floyd (left) and Lee Trevino both posted 68s in the second round.

Trevino made his hay on the back nine. There was just one flaw, a bogey five at the twelfth. His tee shot, as usual, was dead center. "But I was trying to cut a three-wood in, and I cut it too much," he said. He missed the green, chipped to six feet and two-putted. He had three birdies: a twenty-foot putt at the tenth, after a four-iron approach; a twenty-footer at the par-five sixteenth after a lay-up four-iron and pitching wedge approach; and an eighteen-footer at the eighteenth, after a drive and six-iron.

This — after a two-bogey, two-birdie 35 on the front — was a case of requited love.

"I absolutely fell in love with this golf course when I saw it Monday," Trevino said.

He even loved it on Stormy Thursday. "I just came from the British Masters," Trevino said. "We had six days of that stuff." The difference between the two

Second Round

days for him: "I couldn't reach nine, twelve, fourteen or eighteen on Thursday," he said. "Today, they're all reachable."

Whatever awaited him in the next two rounds, it was a different Lee Trevino who won the Open in 1968 at Oak Hill and in 1971 at Merion. That was the pre-back surgery Trevino, the one with the flat swing and the controlled fade. This one is more upright. He favors a surgically repaired back that left him unable to work on his game beyond practice rounds. This one hits fewer fades, sometimes hits hooks. "I prefer my swing of ten or fifteen years ago," he said. "I knew where it was going."

The real Raymond Floyd finally arrived. He turned in a no-bogey 68 for a 143 total and pronounced the balmy day more to his taste. "We were allowed to perform today," he said. "It was more like survival yesterday." He birdied the par-four fourth from eighteen feet after a wedge approach, and the par-three seventeenth with a five-iron and a twenty-foot putt, and he saved par four times. "The key to my round was hitting fairways and greens," he said. "I hit a lot of both, and this course requires that. I played well."

Tom Watson, the 1982 champion, trying to shake a prolonged slump, rallied for two birdies coming home for a 71 and a share of fourth place at 143. He dropped birdie putts of thirty feet at the fourteenth and twenty-five feet at the sixteenth, easing the sting of a three-bogey front nine. "I played a good round of golf — for the last twelve holes," Watson said. "Three shots is not that many, really. I'm sure Greg feels the same way. Still," he added, "I'd rather be in his position than mine."

Whether anyone could make up ground on Norman depended in part, of course, on the weather. Thursday's massacre helped to inflate the scores. The average score dropped from the 77.55 to a mellower 74.01 on Friday and produced this oddity for statistics freaks: the worst-ball score over the two rounds was 133.

The day also produced a few interest-

Ever-accurate Calvin Peete (above) was not much of a factor at Shinnecock Hills, but Tom Watson (next page) threatened at times.

Second Round

ing sidelights. The evening flight to Syracuse had to take off without Joey Sindelar.

Sindelar, 27, a personable third-year pro out of Horseheads, New York, had made a plane reservation for Friday night. It seemed a prudent move. He had shot 81 on Thursday. "If there's one thing worse than missing the cut," Sindelar said, "it's staying in the same town after you miss the cut. It's like staying at the scene of the crime."

What changed his mind was the competitive course record 66 he shot on Friday. It seemed to come from nowhere. The front nine was routine enough — two birdies, two bogeys, par 35. He parred the tenth. And then he erupted into a string of threes — five of them. He started with a two-putt par at the eleventh, then one-putted for birdies from five feet, then fifteen, fifteen and two. After a par five at the sixteenth, he got yet another three, a par at the seventeenth. All told, he had eight threes on his card, five of them birdies. He got up-and-down at the eighteenth, holing a six-foot putt for his par, wrapped up the 66, and called the airline. He had leaped from obscurity to a tie for twenty-fourth with a 147 total going into the third round.

An Open record was tied, but it didn't matter. Danny Edwards, a twelve-year pro from Edmond, Oklahoma, ripped the back nine for a 30. But all it got him was a 69 and a 152 total. And that, as the pros put it, got him the weekend off.

The cut was made at ten-over-par 150, leaving seventy of the original one hundred and fifty-six players for the final two rounds. Among them were Scott Verplank, who was making his professional debut in this Open, and Sam Randolph, the University of Southern California star and the only amateur of the five in the field to make the cut. Verplank, an All-America out of Oklahoma State University, won the 1985 Western Open, becoming the first amateur in thirty-one years to win an official PGA Tour event. He had filed his Open entry as an amateur, won the National Collegiate Athletic Association individual championship and turned pro. Verplank shot 75-72 for 147.

Joey Sindelar's 66 was a 15-shot climb. Payne Stewart (next page) shot four birdies and 68.

86th U.S. Open
Third Round

I think the only mistake I made all day was going up to that spectator.
Greg Norman

People in golf like to think of their game as a gentlemanly pursuit.

Sportsmanship is an integral part of the game at all levels, so much so that the first section of the official Rules of Golf is titled "Etiquette." For the most part, golf has been able to avoid the displays of bad sportsmanship and obnoxious behavior that have beset other sports. Golf galleries have taken their cue from the players; Bobby Jones, Arnold Palmer, Jack Nicklaus and other visible spokesmen for the game have provided examples for golfers and spectators to emulate.

Perhaps that is why Greg Norman, a proponent of golf's rules of gentlemanly conduct, lost his concentration — and his poise — when he was heckled by a young spectator on the fourteenth hole of the third round of the 1986 Open.

Norman had blown a hefty lead at the thirteenth hole. Three full shots. He drove into the rough, ran his approach shot over the green and down under a bush, ran his next back across the green, chipped to four feet, and two-putted for a double-bogey six. Lee Trevino, paired with Norman, had put his seven-iron approach to about two feet and tapped it in for a birdie three. The three-shot swing left Norman and Trevino tied for the lead.

It was quite a crash. Norman had been threatening to run away with the Open. Through the ninth, he held a four-stroke lead on Mark McCumber, who was stirring, and a five-stroke lead on Trevino. He began the day as the only player under par and would finish with a 71, an even-par total of 210, and a one-stroke lead.

Greg Norman was in command until driving into the rough at No. 13.

Third Round

Norman had given up the lead at the thirteenth, and was walking up the fourteenth fairway when a heckler opened up. Norman strode directly over to him. Only the yellow gallery rope separated them. Norman stuck a finger in the man's face. "If you want to say anything to me," he said, "say it after the round when I can say something back. Don't be an ass."

Golf events generally proceed like chamber music concerts. The applause comes only after the performance — polite for a good one, loud for a great one. But demonstrative golf fans are hardly unknown, and they do choose sides. Sometimes their cheers amount to boos.

Seve Ballesteros heard it when he dumped his approach into the pond at the fifteenth at the Masters only two months earlier. He happened to be a very convincing leader at the moment. "They were cheering for the competition," he tried to explain at a Shinnecock press conference. He was being the diplomat, and a fanciful one. No one believed him. The fans were roaring because the way was now clear for a charging Jack Nicklaus to win the Masters. David Graham heard it at the 1985 British Open. He thought the thunder at the final hole at Royal St. George's was for a great shot. When he got to the green and saw his ball snuggled in a bunker, he knew better. A home player, Sandy Lyle, now could win the British Open.

But this was heckling, a slightly different matter. Still, the prevailing sentiment was that Norman — who is certainly familiar with golf spectators — was a bit skittish at this point. And perhaps overly

Greg Norman's approach shot at No. 13 was over the green ...

sensitive. Norman had already agreed, sort of. "I think the only mistake I made all day," Norman said after the round, "was going up to that spectator."

Saturday was another balmy, sunny day of blue skies and zephyrs. Norman set out to wrap up this Open early. He birdied the par-five fifth after coming out of a

Third Round

Greg Norman	71-210
Hal Sutton	66-211
Lee Trevino	69-211
Bob Tway	69-212
Mike Reid	66-213
Mark McCumber	68-213
Payne Stewart	69-213
Raymond Floyd	70-213
Denis Watson	71-213

bunker to five feet, and he put a nine-iron approach to thirty feet at the eighth, and birdied again. He was now three under par. His nearest challenger was Mark McCumber, four back. McCumber shot the front in four-under 31. Trevino made it in par with an eight-foot birdie at the third and a bogey at the ninth, where he put his second over the green.

The round didn't really begin, it turned out, until the back nine.

First off, Norman, who had parred the tenth in Thursday's turbulence, bogeyed it in the sunshine for the second straight day. Then came the jarring double-bogey at the thirteenth. He had handled the tough par four on Thursday, and then played it five-six in the sun. "I promise you," he said, "I'll par ten and thirteen tomorrow." The vow raised memories of Ballesteros winning the 1984 British Open at St. Andrews, where he had bogeyed the seventeenth, the Road Hole, three days running. Facing one last crack at it, he said, "I will par seventeen tomorrow, or I will come back Monday." He didn't have to play on Monday.

Trevino, whose last victory was the 1984 PGA, birdied the eleventh from fifteen feet and the thirteenth from two, and saved par at the fourteenth and sixteenth. He was tied for the Open lead with Nor-

... and he took six to Lee Trevino's birdie-three.

man coming to the eighteenth. He put his tee shot into the rough, then made his big mistake. He tried to reach the green with a four iron, and put the shot into a bunker. He blasted out and two-putted from fifteen feet for the bogey that knocked him out of share of the lead. "I should have used a five iron and just put it short the green, then chipped up," he said.

The error left Trevino tied for second at one-over 211 with Hal Sutton, who had just tied the day-old course record 66. Sutton bogeyed the fifth, then played the last thirteen holes in five under, including the back nine in 31. He birdied the sixth from eight feet, the tenth on a chip shot, the eleventh from three feet, the fifteenth from eight and the seventeenth from twelve. Then Sutton said, "I don't think 66 is a particularly low score on this golf course."

"I'm a late mover," Sutton said, "but at least I did move, finally." He had won the Memorial Tournament just a few weeks earlier. It was his second victory of the year — Phoenix was the first — and the seventh of a glittering career just five years old. It includes the Tournament Players Championship and the PGA, both in 1983.

Back at the halfway point, Norman, leading by three, said that even a ten-stroke lead was not comfortable. Generally, anyone within six of the lead on the final day still has a chance. That meant the final round of the U.S. Open would resemble Long Island's roads on a Sunday evening. Fully twenty other players were at 216 or less — within six strokes of

Hal Sutton (previous page) played the last 13 holes in five under par for 66, while Lee Trevino birdied No. 11 (above) on his way to 69.

Third Round

Mike Reid shot 66 and was three behind.

Norman. The group included Bob Tway, the first-round leader; Mike Reid, who also tied a course record with a 66; Ben Crenshaw, rebounding after an opening 76; Tom Watson, holding steady with 72-71-71—214; and Nicklaus (67) and Ballesteros (68) at 216, along with the Wadkins brothers, Lanny and Bobby.

Raymond Floyd's no-bogey string ended at the sixth hole after twenty-three straight flawless holes. But he bracketed that bogey with birdies at the second and eighth holes and made the turn in 34. What looked like a move died in a hurry on the back nine. He bogeyed the tenth and twelfth, then birdied the fifteenth to finish at even-par 70. His position was strong — three-over 213 and tied for fifth, just three strokes off the lead. He was largely unnoticed, however. He was within striking range, but then, who wasn't?

The Open was anyone's. It might depend on how the spectators would treat Norman, and if treated badly, whether his rabbit ears would twitch.

Amateur Sam Randolph (next page) was congratulated on his 68 by defending champion Andy North.

Scott Verplank was a contender.

Mark McCumber scored a 68.

86th U.S. Open
Fourth Round

Raymond Floyd's third shot to No. 16 for a birdie led to a family portrait with 6-year-old Christina and wife Maria.

I've always prided myself that I handled pressure well. I'm known as a front-runner. There's a lot of pressure up there. But I came from behind in this one.
Raymond Floyd

The 1986 U.S. Open was in Raymond Floyd's pocket about 4:30 p.m. on Sunday, the final day. This was about two hours before it would end. He didn't know it was over. But Maria Floyd did. He wasn't even in the lead. But wives have a way of knowing. She had seen that look in his eyes.

* * *

You sure don't seem nervous, someone said.

Lee Trevino grinned and shot him a glance. "My nerves went with my back," Trevino said.

It was early on the afternoon of Sunday, June 15, Father's Day. The final round of the eighty-sixth U.S. Open was about to spin itself out. It was almost time for the leaders to take the stage. In the locker room in Shinnecock's shingled old clubhouse, those who braced for the final push were alone with themselves, each getting ready in his own way. Hal Sutton, who was tied with Trevino a stroke behind leader Greg Norman, was sitting and gazing silently out the window. Bob Tway, two strokes back, slowly, methodically peeled a banana. It was silent until Trevino arrived. Trevino's way is to talk. When some golf writers dropped by, he talked.

Trevino's message was the everything-to-gain, nothing-to-lose routine. He had both. "I don't give a damn what I shoot," Trevino was saying, "and a man is dangerous when he doesn't give a damn. I'm just glad to be there. I could shoot a thousand, I don't care. People are going to say,

Fourth Round

look at that old SOB — at least he's in there."

Floyd was relaxing on a red-upholstered bench. The best he could offer was a snippet of pragmatism. Trevino was wearing a red jersey and black slacks. Payne Stewart, as always a sonata in pastels, was wearing yellow knickers, a yellow cap, yellow snakeskin shoes. Against such splashes, Floyd was vanilla. "I wear white," he said. "It's going to be hot out there. You wear white when it's hot."

It was about to get very hot. The United States Golf Association was merely dabbling in history when it took this Open to Shinnecock Hills. They hoped they'd have a good Open, as well. This one is a highlights film: Start from the first tee, go to the last putt at the eighteenth and then hand it an Oscar.

The leaders had no sooner hit the course than the Open was tied. Norman parred the first hole, and his playing partner, Hal Sutton, birdied it. Trevino had birdied it in the pairing ahead moments earlier. There was a three-way tie for the lead at even par. Things would become infinitely more complicated a few minutes later. This happened in the last four pairings: Payne Stewart birdied the fifth, and so did Mark McCumber in the group just behind, and so did the

Greg Norman (left) and Hal Sutton were in the final pairing, but couldn't keep the pace.

pairing right behind him, Trevino and Bob Tway, and then so did Sutton. Five men were tied at even par. It was merely a dress rehearsal. The best was yet to come.

Norman was the mystery man. He dropped out of the chase quickly and decisively.

The galleries were polite, and they cheered for him. The acrimony of the fan incident on Saturday was forgotten. "They were the way galleries are supposed to be," he was to say later. He bogeyed the third and the sixth, and he figured just briefly, joining a huge tie with a birdie at the seventh. Then he came apart: three straight bogeys starting at the

86th U.S. Open

Fourth Round

Raymond Floyd	66-279
Lanny Wadkins	65-281
Chip Beck	65-281
Lee Trevino	71-282
Hal Sutton	71-282
Ben Crenshaw	69-283
Payne Stewart	70-283

ninth, and two more later, interrupted by just one birdie. He was a bewildered man. "I went flat," he said. "When I missed that four-footer and made bogey at the sixth, all the emotion went out of me." His cad-

Bob Tway was a contender.

Mark McCumber was a factor through 15.

Fourth Round

die, Pete Bender, who half-scolded him back in the second round, tried everything. "Nothing would light the fuse," Norman said. He blew to a 75 and finished five over at 285, tied for twelfth.

About 4 p.m., nine players were tied for the lead: Norman, Floyd, Sutton, Tway, Stewart, McCumber, Ben Crenshaw, Lanny Wadkins and Chip Beck. Including Trevino, ten players either held or shared the lead through the day.

Wadkins and Beck bombed their way into the picture with 65s, matching the brand-new course record and tying at one-over 281. Joey Sindelar's course-record 66 had lasted for only two rounds. It was topped by the 65 shot early on Sunday by Mark Calcavecchia, a sometime-tour pro, sometime-caddie. Wadkins' was classic, a five-birdie, no-bogey performance. Beck had two bogeys and two birdies on the front, then shot the back nine in five-under 30. He missed a 29, and a 64, when he failed on a four-foot birdie try at the eighteenth. Wadkins had come in about 5 p.m., and it was very possible at that moment that he would win the Open. There were still ten pairings out on the course, and only Payne Stewart, even through the eleventh, was ahead of him. "All I can do is sit around," Wadkins said, "and hope the winds blow like hell."

Mike Calcavecchia was the first of three in with 65.

Floyd was just another name on a nervous leader board. He kept grinding away. His front nine was not exactly the kind that attracts attention. He saved his par four at the third with a six-foot putt. He birdied the par-four fifth, putting a six-iron approach to eight feet. A chip shot saved his par at the sixth, and two putts from the fringe saved his four at the eighth. And at the ninth, he scrambled to his par after driving into the rough. He shot the front in one-under 34 and gained only one stroke on the field. He was trailing by two at the turn. His next adventure would be a battle with Stewart, with whom he was paired.

Floyd parred the tenth, and when he headed through the crush for the eleventh, Maria Floyd, a dark-haired beauty with flashing eyes, caught his eye. She felt better.

"I was a basket case before that," she said. This was the same husband who only a week earlier blew sky-high at Westchester, and you know how that must feel to a guy who's 43 years old in a sea of whippy-backed kids. He needed more than an Open victory. He needed to get his self-esteem back. So she watched him anxiously as he marched by. That's when she knew this Open was history.

ABC Sports used a 150-foot crane.

Payne Stewart came close again.

Lee Trevino tied for fourth place.

Fourth Round

Ben Crenshaw challenged.

She saw "that look," she said.

"His eyes glaze over. You can almost see them bulge," she said. "When he gets that look, they're going to have to go out and beat him."

Even Payne Stewart spotted it. "When he's playing well, you can see it in his eyes," Stewart said. "They got real big and he just focused in on what he was doing."

Nothing was settled at the eleventh. In fact, it was beginning to look like Stewart's Open. Floyd dropped an eighteen-foot putt for a birdie-two. That's the kind of thing that can shake a leader. But Stewart answered him with a birdie of his own, from four feet. Floyd had to scramble for a par at the twelfth. He drove into a bunker, and eventually had to hole a twenty-footer to save his four. Stewart had a twelve-footer left for his birdie, and he got it. He was now one under par for the Open — the only player under par —and he held a one-stroke lead on Sutton, who had birdied the ninth, and a two-stroke lead on Floyd, among others.

Then Stewart broke down. He bogeyed four of the last six holes. The collapse began at the thirteenth. He blew a three-foot par putt, and Floyd birdied. They were tied at even par.

Stewart bogeyed the fourteenth, failing to get up-and-down after over-clubbing on his approach. Floyd, whose approach also rolled over the green, chipped back to five feet and holed his putt for a save. Floyd was the new leader.

The challengers were falling right and left now. Stewart took himself out with bogeys at the sixteenth and eighteenth. He finished with 70-283 and tied for sixth. McCumber double-bogeyed the sixteenth and bogeyed the seventeenth for 71-284 and a tie for eighth with Bob Tway, who double-bogeyed the sixteenth.

Floyd, in some kind of trance, barely knew what was going on around him.

"I didn't realize I was leading till I came off the fifteenth green," he said.

And when did he smell victory?

"When I made birdie at sixteen," he said, "it looked very realistic."

After he dropped that ten-footer at the sixteenth for his birdie four, he was one under par for the Open and leading by two strokes. It would take a miracle to catch him. Trevino got to two over but parred the last two holes. Sutton bogeyed the fifteenth to go to two over, and couldn't scratch better than par the rest of the way, tying Trevino for fourth at 71-282. Crenshaw birdied the fifteenth, but finished par-par-bogey for 69-283 and a share of sixth. Floyd merely needed to par the last two holes, and he did, for a 66 and his second no-bogey round of the Open. It gave him the only sub-par total of the Open, a one-under 279, and a two-stroke victory over Wadkins and Beck. Floyd won $115,000 out of the $700,000 purse.

Except for what Maria Floyd thought she saw in her husband's eyes, Floyd had given slight indication that he was anything but a tag-along until the final nine holes. He had opened with a 75 on Foul Thursday, the worst start by an Open champion since the 76s of Ben Hogan in 1951 and Jack Fleck in 1955 in post-World War II years. That was only five strokes back, but he was tied for 22nd. ("That was when I won the Open," he said, "because I had no feel and still shot 75.") His 68 on Friday helped a tad. It left him four behind. Then the 70 on Saturday lifted him another stroke closer, but he was merely tied for fifth, and there were eight players between him and the lead. In a seventy-two-hole tournament, he had spotted the field about sixty-eight holes. He made only eleven birdies all told, but more to the point, only eight bogeys and one double bogey.

"I've always prided myself that I hand-

Fourth Round

Chip Beck (left) and Lanny Wadkins shot 65s and shared second place, two strokes behind.

led pressure well," Floyd said. "I'm known as a front-runner. There's a lot of pressure up there. But I came from behind in this one."

So Floyd had taken up a heavy pen and written another chapter in the Year of the Oldies. At 43 years and nine months, he was the oldest champion in Open history, replacing Britain's Ted Ray, who was some months younger than that when he won in 1920. It was Floyd's first Open title, his fourth major (he won the Masters in 1976 and the PGA in 1969 and 1982), his first victory of any kind since the 1985 Houston Open, and the twentieth victory of his twenty-four-year career.

The question of age never occurred to Floyd. "I'm 43, but I don't feel 43," Floyd said. "And I never thought before this week that this could be my last shot at winning an Open. But," he said, eyebrows up, "I suppose it could be."

Raymond Floyd acknowledged the applause after holing his putt at No. 18 for the title.

86th U.S. Open
The Champion

We agreed that you have to take something bad and make something good out of it.
                                    Maria Floyd

The scene was the locker room during the World Series of Golf. Raymond Floyd sat easily on the edge of a leather couch, munching leisurely at chicken and salad. A handful of golf writers approached.

"Can we talk some golf, Raymond?" one asked.

"Sorry," Floyd said. "I'm having lunch, and I don't like to talk golf when I'm eating."

Floyd has the reputation of being firm, honest and generally friendly with writers, if in an aloof kind of way, but he also can be testy. The writers turned to leave.

"But we can talk some baseball," Floyd said.

There was not a surprised eye in the bunch. Floyd really knows his baseball, especially if it's spelled C-u-b-s. He even used to suit up and work out with the Chicago Cubs. The writers fell in around him. This was a star golfer they were talking to, but if things had been different earlier in his life, they may have been interviewing him in another kind of World Series locker room.

"I never had much of an amateur career," Raymond Floyd was saying, shortly after he won the 1986 U.S. Open. Which was not surprising, since Floyd was never much of an amateur. When he was growing up in North Carolina, he would play hundred-dollar Nassaus against guys much older. "And beat them," he said.

Raymond Floyd admired his prize.

Everybody was much older. Floyd was 13.

But nobody ever accused him of being a hustler. The presumption must be that if a 13-year-old kid puts up his own $300, he has more than a working knowledge of the game. This Floyd kid, in fact, was a scratch golfer.

Logic says it's only a question of time before this kind of talent heads for the pro tour. But it wasn't that simple. Floyd grew up in Fort Bragg, North Carolina, where his father, L.B. Floyd, was an Army man. A busy kid, Floyd split his time between golf and baseball. But the charm of $300 paydays aside, baseball was his game and the big leagues his goal. It took a golf victory —an amateur one, ironically — to change his mind. In 1960, at age 17, he won the International Jaycee Junior. That settled it.

Floyd turned professional in 1961, and in 1963 joined the pro tour. This was an inspiring time for a young golfer to come out. Arnold Palmer was the king. Jack Nicklaus had arrived, Gary Player and Billy Casper were mighty forces and Doug Sanders a terrific splash of color. It also must have been an intimidating time for a young golfer.

Floyd probably still doesn't know what the word means. Brand-new on the tour, just over 20, he won the 1963 St. Petersburg Open. That was the start of one of golf's most fascinating and durable careers. Also one of the most puzzling.

Floyd's career can be divided into two parts. The dividing line is no more prominent than, say, the Rockies and the way they split the Continental United States.

Not to get too domestic about it, but you can tag them "pre-Maria" and "post-Maria."

Floyd's first big year was 1969, when he won the first of his two PGA Championships and two other tournaments and topped $100,000 in winnings. Then splat. He practically disappeared. He bottomed out at $34,624 in 1972.

No one in golf was all that surprised. It was no secret that Floyd enjoyed a horse race or a social event, even if they happened to be a sudden chartered plane flight from wherever he happened to be playing. He even dropped off the tour for a while and took up life in the North Beach section of San Francisco, hanging out and singing at the night spots.

"Raymond," Lanny Wadkins once said, "has done it all."

Then Floyd met Maria Fraietta in Miami. She is a striking brunette with flashing eyes, a degree from the University of Pennsylvania, and the will of a drill sergeant.

Raymond Floyd had crossed the Great Divide. They were married December 8, 1973.

The miracle didn't take instantly. First, Maria had to get some ground rules down. There was, for example, this lark that Floyd and Bob Rosburg went on. Rosburg, now a television golf commentator but a tour player then, once recounted what Maria had to say to Raymond about that lark: "Either you're a golfer or a horse player. Make up your mind. I thought I had married a golfer."

And so she had, it turned out. Floyd won the 1975 Kemper Open, his first victory in six years. In the 1976 Masters, he had the late Clifford Roberts, Masters chairman, talking to himself. Roberts had ordered certain changes for Augusta National "to protect the integrity of the par fives." Floyd took his five-wood and bashed that integrity silly. He played the fives in fourteen under par, won the Masters by eight strokes, and tied Nicklaus' tournament record of 271. He won his second PGA — his third major — in 1982 at Southern Hills at Tulsa. In the broiling

Floyd The Oldest

At the age of 43 years, eight months and 11 days, Raymond Floyd became the oldest U.S. Open champion. He won his first professional tournament at age 20 years, six months — the fourth youngest.

heat of that August, he simply marched to the front with a 63 and stayed there.

But the U.S. Open forever drove him batty. In his first twenty-one tries, the best he could do was sixth, and that was in 1965. "I wish I knew why," Floyd said at Shinnecock. "I analyzed and I replayed, and I could find no reason. Believe me, if I could, I would have won it long ago."

He was in a tad of a slump coming to Shinnecock. He had not won in over a year, since the 1985 Houston Open. His performance had improved in 1986. But it didn't have a hint of a U.S. Open title in it.

On Friday of Open week, Maria Floyd had to do first things first. She borrowed the Nicklaus jet and flew the boys to summer camp. She left Raymond Jr., 11, at one camp, and Robert, 10, at another. Then she gathered up little Christina, 6, to go watch Daddy win the U.S. Open.

And it all began on a hundred-mile drive a week earlier. Raymond and Maria Floyd were leaving Westchester, heading for Shinnecock. They got all settled down in the car. Then Maria wanted to talk to her husband about bombing out in the Westchester Classic with that 77 in the last round. You're 43, and you're fighting a tidal wave of whippy-backed kids, and your wife wants to talk failure? Floyd wasn't having any.

"I didn't want to talk about it at first," he admitted.

But Maria is not one to be put off easily. Besides, where could he hide?

"We agreed," Maria said — she's got a great grin — "that you have to take something bad and make something good out of it."

Sometimes there's nothing like a nice family chat.

86th U.S. Open
Statistics

Hole	1	2	3	4	5	6	7	8	9	10	11	12	13	14	15	16	17	18	Total	
Par	4	3	4	4	5	4	3	4	4	4	3	4	4	4	4	5	3	4	70	
Raymond Floyd																				
Round 1	4	3	5	5	5	4	3	4	6	4	2	5	3	5	4	5	3	5	75	
Round 2	4	3	4	3	5	4	3	4	4	4	3	4	4	4	4	5	2	4	68	
Round 3	4	2	4	4	5	5	3	3	4	5	3	5	4	4	3	5	3	4	70	
Round 4	4	3	4	3	5	4	3	4	4	4	2	4	3	4	4	4	3	4	66	279
Lanny Wadkins																				
Round 1	5	3	5	4	5	4	2	4	6	4	3	4	4	4	3	5	5	4	74	
Round 2	5	3	4	5	5	4	3	3	5	4	2	5	4	3	4	4	3	4	70	
Round 3	3	3	4	4	5	4	4	3	6	4	3	4	5	4	3	6	3	4	72	
Round 4	4	2	4	4	5	4	3	4	4	4	2	4	3	3	4	4	3	4	65	281
Chip Beck																				
Round 1	4	3	4	5	5	4	3	4	5	4	2	4	5	5	4	5	4	5	75	
Round 2	4	3	3	4	4	6	3	4	5	4	3	4	3	6	4	5	4	4	73	
Round 3	4	3	4	4	5	4	3	4	4	4	4	4	3	4	3	5	2	4	68	
Round 4	4	3	4	3	6	5	2	4	4	3	2	3	3	4	3	5	3	4	65	281

Hole	Par	Avg.	Eagles	Birdies	Pars	Bogeys	Double Bogeys	Higher	Min.	Max.	Rank
1	4	4.025	1	70	301	69	7	0	2	6	16
2	3	3.321	0	26	270	135	16	1	2	6	7
3	4	4.397	0	32	242	144	25	5	3	8	5
4	4	4.281	0	38	274	114	17	5	3	8	10
5	5	5.007	3	96	263	70	13	3	3	8	18
6	4	4.491	0	20	221	181	19	7	3	7	2
7	3	3.286	0	37	273	114	22	2	2	7	9
8	4	4.105	1	61	290	84	10	2	2	7	14
9	4	4.422	0	33	215	179	20	1	3	7	4
OUT	35	37.335	5	413	2349	1090	149	26	30	47	
10	4	4.451	0	25	243	139	36	5	3	8	3
11	3	3.228	0	48	272	107	20	1	2	6	11
12	4	4.375	0	33	243	146	23	3	3	7	6
13	4	4.210	0	63	246	125	12	2	3	9	12
14	4	4.321	1	45	255	116	20	11	2	9	7
15	4	4.145	0	59	281	93	14	1	3	7	13
16	5	5.022	1	91	273	65	16	2	3	8	17
17	3	3.083	0	57	306	77	7	1	2	6	15
18	4	4.509	0	22	219	170	34	3	3	9	1
IN	35	37.344	2	443	2338	1038	182	29	30	47	
TOTAL	70	74.679	7	856	4687	2128	331	55	65	88	

U.S. Open Past Results

Date	Winner, Runner-Up	Score	Site	Entry
1895 (Oct.)	**Horace Rawlins** Willie Dunn	173 175	**Newport G.C.,** Newport, R.I.	11
1896 (July)	**James Foulis** Horace Rawlins	†152 155	**Shinnecock Hills G.C.,** Southampton, N.Y.	35
1897 (Sept.)	**Joe Lloyd** Willie Anderson	162 163	**Chicago G.C.,** Wheaton, Ill.	35
1898 (June)	**Fred Herd** Alex Smith	328 335	**Myopia Hunt Club,** S. Hamilton, Mass.	49
1899 (Sept.)	**Willie Smith** George Low/Val Fitzjohn/W.H. Way	315 326	**Baltimore C.C.,** (Roland Park Course) Baltimore, Md.	81
1900 (Oct.)	**Harry Vardon** J.H. Taylor	313 315	**Chicago G.C.,** Wheaton, Ill	60
1901 (June)	**Willie Anderson** Alex Smith	331-85 331-86	**Myopia Hunt Club,** S. Hamilton, Mass.	60
1902 (Oct.)	**Lawrence Auchterlonie** Stewart Gardner/*Walter J. Travis	307 313	**Garden City G.C.,** Garden City, N.Y.	90
1903 (June)	**Willie Anderson** David Brown	307-82 307-84	**Baltusrol G.C.,** (original course) Springfield, N.J.	89
1904 (July)	**Willie Anderson** Gilbert Nicholls	303 308	**Glen View Club,** Golf, Ill.	71
1905 (Sept.)	**Willie Anderson** Alex Smith	314 316	**Myopia Hunt Club,** S. Hamilton, Mass.	83
1906 (June)	**Alex Smith** William Smith	295 302	**Onwentsia Club,** Lake Forest, Ill.	68
1907 (June)	**Alex Ross** Gilbert Nicholls	302 304	**Philadelphia Cricket C.,** (St. Martins Course) Philadelphia, Pa.	82
1908 (Aug.)	**Fred McLeod** Willie Smith	322-77 322-83	**Myopia Hunt Club,** S. Hamilton, Mass.	88
1909 (June)	**George Sargent** Tom McNamara	290 294	**Englewood G.C.,** Englewood, N.Y.	84
1910 (June)	**Alex Smith** John J. McDermott Macdonald Smith	298-71 298-75 298-77	**Philadelphia Cricket C.,** (St. Martins Course) Philadelphia, Pa.	75
1911 (June)	**John J. McDermott** Michael J. Brady George O. Simpson	307-80 307-82 307-85	**Chicago G.C.,** Wheaton, Ill.	79
1912 (Aug.)	**John J. McDermott** Tom McNamara	294 296	**C.C. of Buffalo,** Buffalo, N.Y.	131
1913 (Sept.)	***Francis Ouimet** Harry Vardon Edward Ray	304-72 304-77 304-78	**The Country Club,** Brookline, Mass.	165
1914 (Aug.)	**Walter Hagen** *Charles Evans, Jr.	290 291	**Midlothian C.C.,** Blue Island, Ill.	129
1915 (June)	***Jerome D. Travers** Tom McNamara	297 298	**Baltusrol G.C.,** (original course) Springfield, N.J.	141
1916 (June)	***Charles Evans, Jr.** Jock Hutchison	286 288	**Minikahda Club,** Minneapolis, Minn.	94
1917-18 — No Championships: World War I				
1919 (June)	**Walter Hagen** Michael J. Brady	301-77 301-78	**Brae Burn C.C.,** West Newton, Mass.	142
1920 (Aug.)	**Edward Ray** Harry Vardon/Jack Burke, Sr./Leo Diegel/Jock Hutchison	295 296	**Inverness Club,** Toledo, Ohio	265
1921 (July)	**James M. Barnes** Walter Hagen/Fred McLeod	289 298	**Columbia C.C.,** Chevy Chase, Md.	262
1922 (July)	**Gene Sarazen** *Robert T. Jones, Jr./John L. Black	288 289	**Skokie C.C.,** Glencoe, Ill.	323
1923 (July)	***Robert T. Jones, Jr.** Bobby Cruickshank	296-76 296-78	**Inwood C.C.,** Inwood, N.Y.	360
1924 (June)	**Cyril Walker** *Robert T. Jones, Jr.	297 300	**Oakland Hills C.C.,** (South Course) Birmingham, Mich.	319
1925 (June)	**William Macfarlane** *Robert T. Jones, Jr.	291-75-72 291-75-73	**Worcester C.C.,** Worcester, Mass.	445

Past Results

Date	Winner, Runner-Up	Score	Site	Entry
1926 (June)	***Robert T. Jones, Jr.** Joe Turnesa	293 294	**Scioto C.C.,** Columbus, Ohio	694
1927 (June)	**Tommy Armour** Harry Cooper	301-76 301-79	**Oakmont C.C.,** Oakmont, Pa.	898
1928 (June)	**Johnny Farrell** *Robert T. Jones, Jr.	294-143 294-144	**Olympia Fields C.C.,** (No. 4 Course) Mateson, Ill.	1,064
1929 (June)	***Robert T. Jones, Jr.** Al Espinosa	294-141 294-164	**Winged Foot G.C.,** (West Course) Mamaroneck, N.Y.	1,000
1930 (July)	***Robert T. Jones, Jr.** Macdonald Smith	287 289	**Interlachen C.C.,** Minneapolis, Minn.	1,177
1931 (July)	**Billy Burke** George Von Elm	292-149-148 292-149-149	**Inverness Club,** Toledo, Ohio	1,141
1932 (June)	**Gene Sarazen** Bobby Cruickshank/T. Philip Perkins	286 289	**Fresh Meadow C.C.,** Flushing, N.Y.	1,011
1933 (June)	***John Goodman** Ralph Guldahl	287 288	**North Shore C.C.,** Glenview, Ill	915
1934 (June)	**Olin Dutra** Gene Sarazen	293 294	**Merion Cricket C.,** (East Course) Ardmore, Pa.	1,063
1935 (June)	**Sam Parks, Jr.** Jimmy Thomson	299 301	**Oakmont C.C.,** Oakmont, Pa	1,125
1936 (June)	**Tony Manero** Harry Cooper	282 284	**Baltusrol G.C.,** (Upper Course) Springfield, N.J.	1,277
1937 (June)	**Ralph Guldahl** Sam Snead	281 283	**Oakland Hills C.C.,** (South Course) Birmingham, Mich.	1,402
1938 (June)	**Ralph Guldahl** Dick Metz	284 290	**Cherry Hills C.C.,** Englewood, Colo.	1,223
1939 (June)	**Byron Nelson** Craig Wood Denny Shute	284-68-70 284-68-73 284-76	**Philadelphia C.C.,** (Spring Mill Course) West Conshohocken, Pa.	1,193
1940 (June)	**Lawson Little** Gene Sarazen	287-70 287-73	**Canterbury, G.C.,** Cleveland, Ohio	1,161
1941 (June)	**Craig Wood** Denny Shute	284 287	**Colonial Club,** Fort Worth, Tex.	1,048
1942-45 — No Championships: World War II				
1946 (June)	**Lloyd Mangrum** Byron Nelson/Victor Ghezzi	284-72-72 284-72-73	**Canterbury, G.C.,** Cleveland, Ohio	1,175
1947 (June)	**Lew Worsham** Sam Snead	282-69 282-70	**St. Louis C.C.,** Clayton, Mo.	1,356
1948 (June)	**Ben Hogan** Jimmy Demaret	276 278	**Riviera C.C.,** Los Angeles, Calif.	1,411
1949 (June)	**Cary Middlecoff** Sam Snead/Clayton Heafner	286 287	**Medinah C.C.,** (No. 3 Course) Medinah, Ill.	1,348
1950 (June)	**Ben Hogan** Lloyd Mangrum George Fazio	287-69 287-73 287-75	**Merion G.C.,** (East Course) Ardmore, Pa.	1,379
1951 (June)	**Ben Hogan** Clayton Heafner	287 289	**Oakland Hills C.C.,** (South Course) Birmingham, Mich.	1,511
1952 (June)	**Julius Boros** Ed (Porky) Oliver	281 285	**Northwood Club,** Dallas, Tex.	1,688
1953 (June)	**Ben Hogan** Sam Snead	283 289	**Oakmont, C.C.,** Oakmont, Pa.	1,669
1954 (June)	**Ed Furgol** Gene Littler	284 285	**Baltusrol G.C.,** (Lower Course) Springfield, N.J.	1,928
1955 (June)	**Jack Fleck** Ben Hogan	287-69 287-72	**Olympic Club,** (Lake Course) San Francisco, Calif.	1,522
1956 (June)	**Cary Middlecoff** Julius Boros/Ben Hogan	281 282	**Oak Hill C.C.,** (East Course) Rochester, N.Y.	1,921
1957 (June)	**Dick Mayer** Cary Middlecoff	282-72 282-79	**Inverness Club,** Toledo, Ohio	1,907
1958 (June)	**Tommy Bolt** Gary Player	283 287	**Southern Hills C.C.,** Tulsa, Okla.	2,132
1959 (June)	**Bill Casper, Jr.** Bob Rosburg	282 283	**Winged Foot G.C.,** (West Course) Mamaroneck, N.Y.	2,385
1960 (June)	**Arnold Palmer** *Jack Nicklaus	280 282	**Cherry Hills C.C.,** Englewood, Colo.	2,453
1961 (June)	**Gene Littler** Doug Sanders/Bob Goalby	281 282	**Oakland Hills C.C.,** (South Course) Birmingham, Mich.	2,449

86th U.S. Open

Date	Winner, Runner-Up	Score	Site	Entry
1962 (June)	**Jack Nicklaus** Arnold Palmer	283-71 283-74	**Oakmont C.C.,** Oakmont, Pa.	2,475
1963 (June)	**Julius Boros** Jacky Cupit Arnold Palmer	293-70 293-73 293-76	**The Country Club,** Brookline, Mass.	2,392
1964 (June)	**Ken Venturi** Tommy Jacobs	278 282	**Congressional C.C.,** Washington, D.C.	2,341
1965 (June)	**Gary Player** Kel Nagle	282-71 282-74	**Bellerive C.C.,** St. Louis, Mo.	2,271
1966 (June)	**Bill Casper, Jr.** Arnold Palmer	278-69 278-73	**Olympic Club,** (Lake Course) San Francisco, Calif.	2,475
1967 (June)	**Jack Nicklaus** Arnold Palmer	275 279	**Baltusrol G.C.,** (Lower Course) Springfield, N.J.	2,651
1968 (June)	**Lee Trevino** Jack Nicklaus	275 279	**Oak Hill C.C.,** (East Course) Rochester, N.Y.	3,007
1969 (June)	**Orville Moody** Deane Beman/Al Geiberger/Bob Rosburg	281 282	**Champions G.C.,** (Cypress Creek Course) Houston, Tex.	3,397
1970 (June)	**Tony Jacklin** Dave Hill	281 288	**Hazeltine National G.C.,** Chaska, Minn.	3,605
1971 (June)	**Lee Trevino** Jack Nicklaus	280-68 280-71	**Merion G.C.,** (East Course) Ardmore, Pa.	4,279
1972 (June)	**Jack Nicklaus** Bruce Crampton	290 293	**Pebble Beach G.L.,** Pebble Beach, Calif.	4,196
1973 (June)	**John Miller** John Schlee	279 280	**Oakmont C.C.,** Oakmont, Pa.	3,580
1974 (June)	**Hale Irwin** Forrest Fezler	287 289	**Winged Foot G.C.,** (West Course) Mamaroneck, N.Y.	3,914
1975 (June)	**Lou Graham** John Mahaffey	287-71 287-73	**Medinah C.C.,** (No. 3 Course) Medinah, Ill.	4,214
1976 (June)	**Jerry Pate** Tom Weiskopf/Al Geiberger	277 279	**Atlanta Athletic C.,** Duluth, Ga.	4,436
1977 (June)	**Hubert Green** Lou Graham	278 279	**Southern Hills C.C.,** Tulsa, Okla.	4,608
1978 (June)	**Andy North** J.C. Snead/Dave Stockton	285 286	**Cherry Hills C.C.,** Englewood, Colo.	4,897
1979 (June)	**Hale Irwin** Gary Player/Jerry Pate	284 286	**Inverness Club,** Toledo, Ohio	4,853
1980 (June)	**Jack Nicklaus** Isao Aoki	†272 274	**Baltusrol G.C.,** (Lower Course) Springfield, N.J.	4,812
1981 (June)	**David Graham** Bill Rogers/George Burns	273 276	**Merion G.C.,** (East Course) Ardmore, Pa.	4,946
1982 (June)	**Tom Watson** Jack Nicklaus	282 284	**Pebble Beach G.L.,** Pebble Beach, Calif.	5,255
1983 (June)	**Larry Nelson** Tom Watson	280 281	**Oakmont C.C.,** Oakmont, Pa.	5,039
1984 (June)	**Fuzzy Zoeller** Greg Norman	276-67 276-75	**Winged Foot G.C.,** (West Course) Mamaroneck, N.Y.	5,195
1985 (June)	**Andy North** Chen Tze-Chung/Denis Watson/Dave Barr	279 280	**Oakland Hills C.C.,** (South Course) Birmingham, Mich.	5,274
1986 (June)	**Raymond Floyd** Lanny Wadkins/Chip Beck	279 281	**Shinnecock Hills G.C.,** Southampton, N.Y.	§5,410

† Record Score   * Denotes Amateur   § Record Entry

1917—An Open Patriotic Tournament was conducted by the USGA for the benefit of the American Red Cross at the Whitemarsh Valley Country Club, Philadelphia, Pa., June 20-22. Winner: Jock Hutchison, 292; runner-up: Tom McNamara, 299.

1942—A Hale America Tournament was conducted by the USGA in cooperation with the Chicago District Golf Association and the Professional Golfers' Association of America for the benefit of the Navy Relief Society and the United Service Organization at Ridgemoor Country Club, Chicago, Ill., June 18-21. Winner: Ben Hogan, 271; runners-up: Jimmy Demaret and Mike Turnesa, 274.

U.S. Open Championship Records

Amateurs: Champions — Francis Ouimet (1913); Jerome D. Travers (1915); Charles Evans, Jr. (1916); Robert T. Jones, Jr. (1923-26-29-30); John Goodman (1933).

Amateurs: Lowest 18-Hole Score — 65 by James B. McHale in third round in 1947, and James Simons in third round in 1971.

Amateurs: Lowest 72-Hole Scores — 282 by Jack Nicklaus in 1960; 283, James Simons in 1971.

Best Comebacks — 18 Holes: Jack Fleck in 1955 was nine strokes off the pace and came back to win.

36 Holes — Lou Graham in 1975 was 11 strokes behind.

54 Holes — Arnold Palmer in 1960 was seven strokes behind. John Miller in 1973 was six strokes behind.

63 Holes — Billy Casper was seven strokes behind Arnold Palmer with nine holes to play in 1966. Casper shot 32 on the incoming nine, Palmer shot 39.

Best Start by Champion — 63 by Jack Nicklaus in 1980.

Best Finish by Champion — 63 by John Miller in 1973. Second low is 65 by Arnold Palmer in 1960, Jack Nicklaus in 1967 and Fuzzy Zoeller in a playoff in 1984.

Champions Who Led All the Way — Only four have led after every round — Walter Hagen in 1914, Jim Barnes in 1921, Ben Hogan in 1953 and Tony Jacklin in 1970. Seven other champions have led or were in a tie all the way — Willie Anderson in 1903, Alex Smith in 1906, Charles Evans, Jr., in 1916, Tommy Bolt in 1958, Jack Nicklaus in 1972 and 1980, and Hubert Green in 1977.

Clubs Most Often Host — Baltusrol Golf Club, Springfield, N.J., and Oakmont Country Club, Oakmont, Pa., six times. Opens were played at Baltusrol in 1903, 1915, 1936, 1954, 1967 and 1980, and at Oakmont in 1927, 1935, 1953, 1962, 1973 and 1983. Oakland Hills Country Club, Birmingham, Mich., has been host to the Open five times, in 1924, 1937, 1951, 1961 and 1985.

Consecutive Winners — Five players: Willie Anderson (1903-04-05); John J. McDermott (1911-12); Robert T. Jones, Jr. (1929-30); Ralph Guldahl (1937-380) and Ben Hogan (1950-51).

Entry Record — 5,410 in 1986.

Finishes in First Ten — 18 by Jack Nicklaus. Walter Hagen finished in the first ten 16 times; Ben Hogan 15 times.

First Score in 60s — David Hunter, of Essex County Club, West Orange, N.J., returned a card of 68 in the first round of the 1909 Championship. He finished with 313 and in a tie for 30th.

Foreign Winners — David Graham, of Australia, became the 20th foreign-born winner in 1981. However, 16 of the 20 had already emigrated to the United States before they won. The four overseas champions were Harry Vardon of England in 1900, Ted Ray of England in 1920, Gary Player of South Africa in 1965, and Tony Jacklin of England in 1970.

Foreign Players' Best 72-Hole Scores — 273 — David Graham in 1981; 274 — Isao Aoki in 1980; 276 — Greg Norman in 1984; 280 — Chen Tze-Chung, Denis Watson and Dave Barr in 1985; 281 — Tony Jacklin in 1970; 282 — Gary Player and Kel Nagle in 1965, Bobby Locke in 1948.

Highest Scores to Lead Field, 18 Holes — All-time high is 89 by Willie Dunn, James Foulis, and Willie Campbell in 1895. Since World War II, high is 71 in 1951, 1958, 1970 and 1972.

Highest Scores to Lead Field, 36 Holes — All-time high is 173 by Horace Rawlins in 1895. (This was a 36-hole Open.) Since World War II, high is 144 in 1951, 1955 and 1972.

Highest Scores to Lead Field, 54 Holes — All-time high is 249 by Stewart Gardner in 1901. Since World War II, high is 218 in 1951 and 1963.

Highest Scores to Lead Field, 72 Holes — All-time high is 331 by Willie Anderson and Alex Smith in 1901; Anderson won the playoff. More recent high is 299 by Sam Parks, Jr., in 1935. The post-World War II high is 293 by Julius Boros, Jacky Cupit and Arnold Palmer in 1963; Boros won the playoff.

Highest 72-Hole Score — Professional John

Harrison, 393, in 1900.

Highest 36-Hole Cut — 155 in 1955 (low 50 and ties).

Lowest 9-Hole Score — 30 by Danny Edwards on the second nine of the second round in 1986; by Lennie Clements on the first nine of the third round in 1986; by Chip Beck on the second nine of the fourth round in 1986; by George Burns on the first nine of the second round in 1982; by Raymond Floyd on the first nine of the first round in 1980; by Tom Shaw in the first round and Bob Charles in the last round in 1971, both on the first nine; by Steve Spray on the second nine of the fourth round in 1968; by Ken Venturi on the first nine of the third round in 1964; by Arnold Palmer on the first nine of the final round in 1960; and by amateur James B. McHale, Jr., on the first nine in the third round in 1947.

Lowest Round — 63 by Jack Nicklaus and Tom Weiskopf (first round) over the Lower Course of the Baltusrol Golf Club, Springfield, N.J., in 1980; by John Miller (final round) at Oakmont Country Club, Oakmont, Pa., in 1973.

Lowest First Round — 63 by Jack Nicklaus and Tom Weiskopf, at the Baltusrol Golf Club, Springfield, N.J., in 1980.

Lowest Second Round — 64 by Tommy Jacobs, Congressional Country Club, Bethesda, Md., in 1964; by Rives McBee, Olympic Club, San Francisco, in 1966.

Lowest Third Round — 64 by Ben Crenshaw, Merion Golf Club, Ardmore, Pa., in 1981.

Lowest Fourth Round — 63 by John Miller, Oakmont (Pa.) Country Club, in 1973.

Lowest First 36 Holes — 134 by Jack Nicklaus in 1980 and Chen Tze Chung in 1985.

Lowest Last 36 Holes — 132 by Larry Nelson in 1983.

Lowest First 54 Holes — 203 by George Burns in 1981 and Chen Tze Chung in 1985. 204 by Jack Nicklaus and Isao Aoki in 1980.

Lowest Last 54 Holes — 204 by Jack Nicklaus in 1967.

Lowest 36-Hole Cut — 146 in 1980 and 1985 (low 60 and ties); 147 in 1960 (low 50 and ties).

Lowest 72-Hole Scores — 272 — Jack Nicklaus (63-71-70-68) in 1980; 273 — David Graham (68-68-70-67) in 1981; 274 — Isao Aoki (68-68-68-70) in 1980; 275 — Jack Nicklaus (71-67-72-65) in 1967; and Lee Trevino (69-68-69-69) in 1968.

Most Consecutive Birdies — Six by George Burns, who birdied the second through the seventh holes in the second round at Pebble Beach (Calif.) Golf Links in 1982.

Most Consecutive Opens — Gene Sarazen teed off in 31 successive Opens from 1920 through 1954 (no Championships 1942-45 because of World War II). Arnold Palmer teed off in 31 consecutively from 1953 through 1983. Jack Nicklaus has played in 30 consecutive Opens (1957-1986).

Most Victories — Four men have won four times: Willie Anderson (1901-03-04-05), Robert T. Jones, Jr. (1923-26-29-30), Ben Hogan (1948-50-51-53), Jack Nicklaus (1962-67-72-80).

Most Times Runner-up — Sam Snead, Robert T. Jones, Jr., Arnold Palmer and Jack Nicklaus, four times each.

Most Decisive Victories — 11 strokes — Willie Smith in 1899. Nine strokes — Jim Barnes in 1921.

Most Sub-Par Rounds in Career — 29 by Jack Nicklaus; 18 by Ben Hogan; 17 by Sam Snead and Lee Trevino.

Most Rounds Under 70 in Career — 24 by Jack Nicklaus; 15 by Arnold Palmer; Ben Hogan had 14.

Most Strokes on One Hole — Ray Ainsley took 19 strokes on the par-four sixteenth in the second round at the Cherry Hills Club, Englewood, Colo., in 1938.

Oldest Champion — Raymond Floyd was 43 years, eight months and 11 days old, when he won in 1986; Ted Ray was 43 years, four months and 16 days old, when he won in 1920; Julius Boros, the third oldest, was 26 days younger than Ted Ray on the day he won the Championship in 1963.

Pace-Setters with Largest Leads, 18 Holes — Five strokes — Tommy Armour in 1933.

Pace-Setters with Largest Leads, 36 Holes — Five strokes — Willie Anderson in 1903.

Pace-Setters with Largest Leads, 54 Holes — Seven strokes — Jim Barnes in 1921.

Poorest Start for Champion — The all-time high is 91 by Horace Rawlins in 1895. The post-World War II high is 76 by Ben Hogan in 1951 and Jack Fleck in 1955.

Poorest Finish for Champion — All-time high is 84 by Fred Herd in 1898. The post-World War II high is 75 by Cary Middlecoff in 1949.

Youngest Champion — John J. McDermott was 19 years, 10 months and 14 days old when he won in 1911.